Toxic America: Broken Barriers

Volume 5

Authored by Bobby Simonds

ISBN: 1724404490

ISBN 13: 9781724404497

Library of Congress Control Number: **XXXXX**

LCCN Imprint Name: **City and State**

bobby.simonds@gmail.com

www.facebook.com/bobbyraysimonds

www.facebook.com/bobbyrsimonds

www.instagram.com/@bobbysimonds

#bobbyraysimonds

#bobbysimonds

#BOBBYRAYSIMONDS

#ATWISTINTRAVEL

#risenfromtheashes

#toxicamerica

#Challenge-thyself

#avoidinghavoc

1

Since 1998, we have been witnessing a rise with school shootings. It has been a constant reminder with how deadly, guns can be...in the wrong hands.

They say "guns kill people." But in reality, ***People kill people, by using guns.***

Since the beginning of crime, we often see retaliation with civilians against the Police. We also often see why. Police are constantly hurting people - both armed, and unarmed people. And in the ghetto, we witness *Police Brutality* for no apparent reason, other than racism.

In the 1950s and 1960s, America had fought for *Equal Civil Rights.* Nowadays, we continue to fight for the same rights. Even though *Martin Luther King, Jr., and Malcolm X (and others)*, had fought long and hard to make these rights written and passed within the *Constitutional Rights (and Civil Rights),* we still see both *Blacks & White* wars in America - amongst other countries. It seems to me that Human Rights are an ongoing Illusion...

Since 2000, we have had access to many various gadgets, with only a click or finger away from accessing the internet.

With the technological advances in the past couple of decades, there has been many rumors - and proof - online, containing clones (a.k.a., Artificial Intelligence).

Once, we had fell upon an invention with the television (over half a century ago); which sucked our minds dry...with pretty colors, and pictures!

Now, it's all about the tablets and smart phones. Three hours of our daily lives can easily be drained from these damn devices. And all for what? The more we use them, the more likely we become distracted away from our personal lives - with texting, and the use of social media, by sharing things to another person just with a few simple procedures.

We have become dependent with these smart phones for remembering contact information, music, video streaming, research, social "gatherings", event planners, and much more.

There had once been a time before these various gadgets, that we actually had an attention span of more than ten seconds at a time. We also were forced to use our memories; let alone we were surprised to hear from people with who was calling us, because we didn't have "caller-ID."

Brainstorming once had been about using our minds, rather than using *Google, Wikipedia, Youtube.com, Yahoo!,* and other resources.

Thanks to the "Smart" technology, you can now receive this inside your automobile for an added feature; even appliances & home/office security are even offering the same technology, and features.

In the last 2-3 years, 5G towers began popping up all over America. Which creates radio frequencies that "communicate" with various parts of the human body. From what I gather, this would include, but not limited to: *the human brain, liver, blood flow (veins), the nervous system, and even the human heart.*

The 5G tower also has been proven to cause many various types of cancers in a short period of time, if contact is too close. In some studies, it only takes up to 25 feet from the tower, for a human (or animal). Some people have even mentioned the radiation concern with being closer than 25 feet to the towers. Can you imagine the fees for health insurance for the workers that have to put these towers together;

which many of these workers aren't aware of the high health risks?

Supposedly, the purpose of the 5G towers was to better support internet speed, both WI-FI and LAN lines. It is also supposed to improve the speed of cell phones accessing your data options - including the internet, and various apps.

There have even been many warnings from technicians telling people to shut off their WI-FI boxes at home after use, because of the hazardous health risks.

Clearly, with these technological advances, there are many

various hazardous health risks. Not just physical, but mental too.

For a young boy, it is all about the latest video game console, moving on up to Virtual Reality. But how safe were/are these games? I love & loved my video games. I still enjoy a good kick-ass game. And I am even a huge fan of the old *Battlefield, Need for Speed, World of Warcraft, Gran Turismo, and even the GTA (Grand Theft Auto)* games. Interaction with killing time, used to be a big part of my...life.

But obviously, it takes up a big portion of ones' life. Not just a child, or teen, but even adulthood. ***No school: Games. No work: games. Empty house: games. Bad weather: Games!*** Clearly, I'm not the only one. After all, look outside once in a while, where's all the kids that should be playing outside on a nice, sunny day?

2

With Texas's recent school shooting, I feel that I must cover a chapter about the issues at hand. I don't mean for the victim's, but for the shooter, and his family.

Leading up to the shooting, there were signs - there almost always are. Two days after the shooting, what the media didn't cover - per usual - is all the police reports leading up to the shooting. There was approximately 30 various times that the police were at the shooters' home, and even the FBI had been made aware of a Youtube video that this person had created prior to the shooting. ***<u>Dimitiros Pagourtzis</u>*** *had killed 10, and 10 more wounded - according to* **USA TODAY;** *as the student of* **Santa Fe High School (May 18th, 2018), Santa Fe, Texas, is charging him as an adult, with capital murder & aggravated assault of a peace officer.**

This student had given warning before his horrific actions prior to committing these various crimes, and yet, nobody did anything. Were *they* in fear of losing their jobs at the school? Did the FBI not feel that this *Person of Clear Interest* have no *real* intent to harm? What is wrong with society today? **EVERYTHING.**

Between social media, media, and the power of the bully at school, and online, the world has to be looked at with a more open-minded scholar - clearly. The world in the technological age, is harming more and more students all around the world - but especially in America. What has gone so wrong with these youngsters that they feel the end has to go out with such a bang? And if they don't commit murder, they commit suicide? There is obviously something major occurring with today's' youth's, in which, needs changing.

In previous books, I have made it more than clear, that our school system is not only corrupted, but quite harmful for any student with both low self-esteem, but also with depression. This isn't news to me, nor it should be with any rational person, either. Nevertheless, I have also mentioned previously, with every school shooting, comes the rants of *Gun Control*. What we need is *People Control.* Because when people don't understand the situation - whether it's due to them being in denial, or just straight up ignorant - people would rather blame the government for not cracking down harder on gun control.

Gun control, isn't the issue. There are many gun owners - with children - without an incident, such as, a school shooting. The issue isn't mental health either. It's depression, with social media, and bullying. This isn't new, yet, nobody is getting that these are the 3 keys to a massive school shooting, and/or suicide.

Is society so misdirected, that they will never see these factors? Is it like the possibility of Aliens being real? Let's say Aliens exist (because you'd be ignorant not realizing this); then let's look at the Religious believer. What do they call Aliens? Demons, or fallen Angels.

Now, let us take these same religious believers, and put them in the mix of gossip about a school shooting. What do they claim? *The child isn't allowing God into their life.* This is bullshit. Religion has nothing to do with either circumstance. Your faith is blinding you, in which, it's also misdirecting you from the truth, because you begin to sound like an ass on open, social media!

Now for the atheist. It's okay to not trust the media, religion, and even the government for when these sad incidents occur. Because clearly, in these departments, they make no difference, good or bad.

3

Since I am not an actual journalist, I would like to include in this chapter, something I wrote last year; which I created an article for a book, which I scrapped. Nonetheless, it has to do with today's society, along with, having a disability.

Working in today's society is difficult enough, with the continuous *Recession* in play, the *unemployment* rate going up & down, and now with the worries with the upcoming *Minimum-wage increases*, finding a job is, and can be quite difficult.

If this is something you worry about, you're not alone. All the same, if you're like me, who was born with a disability, you cannot just go out into our society's job-market, and snag any job that is available.

You have to be choosy, and meticulous at the type of job you have to apply for, and with your fingers crossed, you nail that one & only position opening - against the hundreds of applicants in front of you, against all odds!

Now, imagine that you landed a job; let's say: a gas station - with a deli setup, cashiering, and a stock room.

You're the new "guy/gal" and say you are finally getting used to the position, your body is struggling to keep up, you need the money, but you have to insist on cutting your hours, just because of your constant, everyday struggles! Then what?

It's certainly difficult enough to work 12-15 hours a week. Especially, when everyone talks smack to you and even around you. You're attempting to bite your tongue, when everyone around you - clearly who has no disabilities - constantly complains about how they're sore & tired; and clearly have no idea the reason why, you, yourself, is struggling to keep up - like a normal individual.

The problem with being born with a disability, or even receiving one later in life; is that there are two major types of disabilities. The first type of disability is *Visual;* the second, *Non-Visual.* If you're anything like me, I have a non-visual disability.

It sucks, and it makes my life a million times more difficult. Not just with working, but living life in the world we are attempting to survive within.

When work is to challenging, because of your disability getting in the way, you have to fight past the denial stage, and look for help. This help would be *Social Supplement Income (S.S.I., State) or Social Security Disability Income (S.S.D.I.; Federal).* And if you are also like me, in denial of owning up to your disability in the first place, and realizing that you aren't like everyone else; and you cannot work, and don't see a doctor regularly - because there is no cure for what you have...Then you struggle to get approved for either *SSI or SSDI!* In the meantime, you see all of the lazy folks who know the *system* too well, who don't deserve a penny thru the state or federal government...

All in all, the person who

deserves the supplemental income is

you, and while you, yourself is being

denied, you know people who are not

only receiving what you should be,

there's nothing you can do!

So how do you survive in an

Unjust Society, with living & surviving

with your non-visual disability? In my

case, I write books, in other cases, you

have to fight harder for what you know

is yours! And while you're fighting to

work harder than everyone else that is

on staff, you are falling further behind

due to your non-visual disability!

It is easier to work in a harsh

environment when you clearly have a *visual* disability. Then the people around you are only annoyed working with someone with a clear, and vivid disability, because they don't have the same peer pressure as everyone else. Not to mention, somebody with a visual handicap is never going to get fired. They may get their hours cut, but they'll never get fired, because the company doesn't want a lawsuit. It doesn't matter how slow that person is!

When I worked at a *McDonald's*, I often laughed when the store manager would get *chewed out* by the owners for not having any one with a visual disability on the staff. The owners would argue, *"While we haven't met our quota, we're required to employ at least one person with a disability; the more handicapped they appear, the better off we look for hiring them!"*

Then the staff would complain if they had to work with that "type" of person, because *they* would slow everyone else down, or get in *their* way. It's sickening and sad at the same time, and just think, that was just at McDonald's. Imagine how it would be at a *Real Job!*

As far as my disability goes; I was born with Mild Cerebral Palsy.

Which is non-visual, and it messes with both my physical body functions, as well as some mental components too. Such as, bad communication skills, grammar, & even comprehensive skills. Which basically means, when I graduated from High School, I was only at an 8th grade reading/writing level.

Just imagine, with leaving school knowing that information, and then fifteen years later, becoming an author! I sure showed them!

As far as work goes, I cannot do it anymore. Even what some would refer to as easy, my body and mind cannot handle it, and as a man, it's humiliating to explain my disability to those who have no idea what I go thru. And I'm constantly hearing, *"Well at least you don't have children..."* Or, *"At least you don't have my disability..."* Or worse, *"Just wait until you're my age..."* As if the last comment has anything to do with me at all!

The biggest downfall of my disability is my low-energy level. I have to have a minimum of 10 cups of coffee or four *Red Bull's* (doesn't matter the size on either) throughout the day, and even then, I struggle to keep up, and keep my eyes open! In addition, my last two doctor's that I did see for updates with my "condition" both agreed that with having Mild Cerebral Palsy, my inner body act's twenty years older.

And so, when I have to hear that damn comment about *Just wait until you're my age*, said by somebody only twenty to thirty years older than me, I want to say, *"I already do know what it's like!"* But I can't, because they won't have a clue as to what I feel like, and they wouldn't understand with not seeing a *visual* disability to begin with!

I'm sorry to say, it won't get any easier, trust me, I know! Best of luck.

4

So, you're thinking about how *easy* it would be to make all that *money* from opening a diner/restaurant?

First off, good luck making a ton of money in the first several years; you'll be barely scraping by with all of your over-head costs. You will be putting more money in the start-up, in comparison of any other business.

Secondly, you must consider the location. Country or city, it all makes a difference. Don't think like an owner, think like a customer on this one!

Thirdly, you must consider your staff. With new establishments, hiring your future staff isn't as easy as *pie.*

Okay, so you think you have it all figured out still?

In this day in age, with beginning a business, you must now accept the fact, that you must create a business that is recession proof. You must secondly consider how much experience you have in the field of business you are willing to start-up. The closer to home (experience in your own personal area of study) it is, the better off you'll be in the long-run. In addition, you must make damn sure that you have enough capital to have this "new" business, taken care of financially for the first two years. Then you must also take into consideration, you will not be able to take any sick days, vacations, or workman's compensation time, if anything were to happen to you. Therefore, you must calculate this into your business plan as well.

Lastly, if you have no experience in what business you would love to create, perhaps you should attend college to get certified. Again, make damn sure it's recession proof.

After all, our economy is like our

gasoline prices: it's all over the place!

5

Believe you and me, I am no expert by far. All the same, I have come a long way with my journey I as a self-published author with both,

Amazon.com & Createspace.com.

With that being said, it is astonishing to see the difference with those whom care about getting the story done right; verses those who just want it out there with sloppy work.

I feel that any time an author makes the time to write down their story, and then proceeds to put it out there for people to read; they should also do so, when it comes to basic to moderate editing. I realize that my editing skills are not at par - even with using MS Word. Nonetheless, you can at least be damn sure to use comma's and periods. I cannot tell you how lazy it looks without having at least a period!

I don't care if your story is about Pie, or another How-to book. If you can make time to write it, & upload it; why can't you squeeze in a little bit extra time with basic editing, or even just fine tuning your story? Why do you feel the need to be in such a rush to upload your book, and make it so unreasonably sloppy?

I've been reading a few free-bees on my kindle lately. I feel like I am a professional compared to some of these people that write a bunch of short story books. This I believe, is partly why there is currently over 8 million authors on Amazon.com, in comparison of 2014, when I had published *A Twist in Travel: Fate - my first book ever!* Back then, there were only 3 to 4 million authors. What a difference. Yet, with today's algorithm technology, you can sell just a few dozen copies and be in the top 100,000 authors!

Did you take the time to realize that if you spend just ten minutes scanning your book, you can easily spot the errors? Why do you feel the need to rush your book?

Some multitude of people feel the need to rush their work. Then the masses believe you should go to college, major in *English*, and assume that college will make you an author. You can't teach natural talent. That's for certain. Obviously, you can however, fine tune it with proper courses.

If somebody without the necessary drive to write, attends college, then graduates...then they proceed to be an author. How do you think their work will turn out? **Forced.**

Non-fiction Kindle authors have

more books than fictional authors – at least in comparison of what I've seen myself. In my personal opinion, they're easier to write, because majority of the time it is being told by the author (nowadays, in a narrative way). Topics like *school shootings, gun control, politics, conspiracies, & religion,* are all heated, emotional debates. Therefore, these topics flow from your mind, thru your fingertips without a second thought.

When it comes to creating fiction, you have to really dig deep within your brain, and it doesn't rush out nearly as fast. I've had 3 novels (fiction), which have taken me more than a year to create. The perfection, the quality, the skill, the knowledge of one's fantasy, takes time, and you truly never know where the book will take you. There are many directions a fictional piece will go - even when creating a plan.

With the millions of books floating around the globe today, it is becoming more & more difficult by the minute to even be noticed. It doesn't matter if you have 500 people on you Facebook-friend's list, or 2000 followers on Twitter, and/or Instagram. Unless you can afford to market your book by paying bundles of money, it is all about word-of-mouth when selling your books online. Both publishers, and Literary Agents are becoming more challenging to impress these days. Let alone, there are more scammers - thanks to the web - and even more of publishers & agents that want your 50-80 percent commission, with you doing majority of the work. It isn't like the 1980s [or earlier] anymore.

I sometimes wish it were like the early to mid-1980s, when internet was not at our fingertips! Just in the last year I only sold 8 paperbacks.

I believe that being an author is one of the greatest achievements that I had made possible in my life - as far as work goes.

I have been told to that I will not make it in this business by a ton of people. Many were the denial letters from various Publishing House's and even Lit. Agents. However, just because I was told "no" a few hundred times in the last year and a half, that doesn't mean diddly to me!

In my experience, people who listen to no are generally the ones that don't want to be something great. These same folks that don't mind settling for no, are also the types of

folks that tell no to everyone they no.

They accept their lives for what they

already have.

Many of the folks I have run

into seem to have no ambition for life.

They want it free, and they expect it.

These same people also don't mind

being the Average Joe! I find this motto

unacceptable. I will not settle for being

at the bottom. I have done it far too

long to accept this to be my life.

I was always told by my

unforgotten father, that I would be the

one to change the stripes in the family.

My Uncle had told me the same thing.

These two-people helped change my way of thinking, even though I heard the word no far too often from even them.

I feel that I will be known in the future as one of the Legendary Writers of the 22nd Century. The problem is that I am still trying to be noticed like The Needle in the Haystack!

I know for a fact that it is only a matter of time. I have completed and released six paperback books in my first year and a half as being an author. I have sold over three hundred digital copies, and roughly two hundred and fifty copies on my own, since my first book went into the

CreateSpace/Amazon market.

Don't get me wrong, that

seems like a low number to most.

However, this is with absolutely no

marketing (aside from the occasional

posting I leave on F.B.). I know that I

will become just as successful as Dean

Koontz, Stephen King, R.L. Stine, and

all of the others. If you had read any of

my books, you have already heard me

say this. However, I know this in my

heart to be true. I don't do it for the

money. Although it would be great to

be rich like these said Novelists or even

somebody as great as Donald Trump;

however, I do this to share my art of writing for the world to enjoy.

For many new authors, they think the best way to go is thru those scam-artists of the Self-Publishing firms. I almost went there myself, but this is not a wise decision.

If you don't know how this business works without a Publisher backing your book(s), then you really need to listen to me. You all need to research on Google or Yahoo! – or whatever search engine you prefer – and research before you make your final decision. Majority of the non-publishing firms are out to steal your money. Money you don't have, because you spent it all on professional editing or a professional cover design company – which I believe is also theft!

What you probably don't realize, is that you can publish your book(s) onto Createspace.com/. Then and only then, you can then upload your book(s) onto **Amazon** for the millions of Kindle users.

This is a great way to test your work for the public. However, it is nearly impossible to get any real money from the digital age. When you price your book for only $2.99, you only receive about a buck a copy! That's way too low. Even when you get lucky enough to sell paperback units on the various online distribution centers, you still only see a few bucks for your fair share of profits. The worst part is, that when you sell these units online you don't make enough to recover from the expenses you had previously spent (and overpaid most likely) with the editing or cover packages offered by *CreateSpace*. It is worth it for when you are new. However, it is a brutal business I cannot express this enough to you all who are thinking of joining the other millions of authors online!

Another thing I can express to you about being a freshman of writing is that when you finally achieve your first book being released, these books of yours will never see the shelf at the various bookstores that sells the thousands of paperback or hardback copies around the globe. These various bookstores – along with the customers – many times over, believes that if you are not published, you are not a true author. These same people that think this way, will never create something unique for people to read!

I believe that many fresh authors have a chance to create

something unique and fresh as I did.

The problem is not so much as you –

the author – it is getting the population

around the globe to get interested

enough to purchase your various books.

6

The term, *dumbing down America*, has often been thrown around to make fun of American's, with other countries world-wide.

Currently, I work at a gas station, as a cashier. I cannot believe the idiocy with people that seem intelligent, until they go to swipe their "card". With having majority of bank & regular credit cards having the "chip" imbedded in them, the masses have become comfortable with card-reader machines only being the "insert" option. My store, currently uses the old swipe method, and then signing the receipt.

It seems to me, that everyone has literally no brain when it comes to the simplest of "cashing-out" experiences. "No, we don't have the chip reader." No, swipe sir/ma'am." "I know, I hate the chip too, yes the government forced the chip upon us." "Yes, sir, the government sucks." These are just a few of my repeated quotes for work. Then there are those that I have to literally ask to see their Driver's License/I.D. card to purchase beer (mandatory at all ages with my store), and then tobacco purchases. I cannot express the crap I have to hear to have the person hand over their identity card to "scan" to be approved to purchase tobacco or alcohol. We had one guy a few weeks after I had started that was so upset that he broke one of the doors on his way out, just because he was carded!

What I attempt to explain to some of these lunatics, is that the government issued you your identification card, and when companies hold your beer hostage, just to see your identity card, who do you think these policies were enforced by? Surely, not the company, this is all government backed. Because "they" want to know that if you want something, you can still *be controlled!*

If you hate our government so much, and don't trust them as much as you claim - you all know who you are - then why do you continue to pay taxes, and reside in this country? Duh, no brainier, they have you by your balls, once you're in, there's no way to escape!

If you continue to reside in America, you fear everything, and just walk around pissed off at the world, for handing you such a "raw-deal". LMFAO. Yeah that's right, I'm laughing at you all. Not because I'm an asshole - partially - but because you all don't know jack shit about how the government works.

When we are all born into this country, the government "forces/encourages" our birth-parents to write down on a form to get our social security "crap" issued. Doing so, we're automatically stuck in the system. They own us right off the bat. "They" also make us get vaccinated - as we all are too familiar with. Vaccinations are a combination of diseases to fight off early childhood diseases. Regardless, they own us, they force us to pay taxes, high gasoline prices, learn shit that they deem fit within our schools. There is so much that is wrong with our country, yet there isn't a better country to live. Majority of us are fully aware of that *catch 22*, yet we still bitch, and we still get nothing corrected. Therefore, stop your belly-aching about handing your identity card to a cashier when you want to purchase alcohol!

7

With research, you come across some strange theories, that is, until you take a moment to consider these various, outlandish (with "normal" people's reality) concepts behind these so-called *outlandish theories.* In the instance I am referring to, is perhaps mainly my own theory, behind all the wars that are claimed to be against another human being. Another word, human verses human wars.

My neighbor had brought to my attention over drinking beer with him (therefore, I just thought it was drunken conversation). I then looked into it, and realized, the deeper I had dug on *Google*, the stranger the story had become. Then I had come across sketches created by the survivors within this story, dated back to the Revolutionary war.

The short version:

The Indians that were fighting against the "white man", were using Druid Magic. They were said to be using Ogres, Fairies, Giants, and other miscellaneous **modern-day fairy tale creatures.**

If this story were true, then it most certainly makes me reconsider even more **Government-Regulated Education.** It really does make perfect sense, especially when speaking of all the wars that we - as a human race - have been involved in.

Consider the last war - that is back in forth - in the middle east. We were all led to believe that it had to do with the 9/11 attacks. Furthermore, it seemed to do with more than guarding the oil, for the oil industries, along with attempting a take-over on these same oil industries - for America, and its allies.

Recently, President Donald Trump signed a "Peace Treaty" with North Korea. This is the first in history, to have been successful. Nonetheless, what's the bigger picture? Is this all a modern-day conspiracy, to fight Aliens? Gaining complete control to have the *New World Order* actually stay in action? Haven't we already been initiated with the *New World Order*? After all, isn't it obvious that electing Presidents around the world a smoke-screen for the true *"world leaders"*?

It is mentioned by many conspirators that there are a 9-man team, setup as the richest of people.

These 9 men, are also said to be "the original blood-line families" from the beginning of humankind. If this is true, then all the Presidents were all puppets for these 9 families. And with that said, they control everything, from then, until now.

If this is all true, then why in the hell aren't we realizing all this shit is a scheme, being set into action, well before any of us are born into this tall-tale world? This brings me back to my previous book, based on the *Simulation Theory*.

Every game has rules, and some of these rules could in fact be our codes imbedded into our real-world-simulation.

Warriors from any time may seem like gigantic gods, but what if all of these fairy tales of giants, fairies, ogres, demons, dinosaurs, and many other strange tales - what Hollywood transformed into movies - were all real? Perhaps from another dimension?

From the 1800s until today, these stories have been long forgotten, and now may seem more or less like fictional stories. Nonetheless, they were passed down from generation to generation, and that only explains to me, that these were stories of truth, and may even carry warnings.

8

Why does it seem like I am the only person coming to this conclusion? Did *they* stamp me as *crazy*, and that is why nobody is listening to me?!

These theories may seem tall-tales from a standpoint, which may seem to the *normal individual* as nutty thinking. But isn't it *nutty* that you don't consider such theories, not to carry crazy thinking, but truthful realities?

Living in the 1900s and even the 2000s, we're lead to believe that science is the only fact. But isn't science created to heal? Investigations

are what we're lead to believe to

discover the truth. Hypothesis is the

only fact, theory is based on a conjured

notion that something is thought to be

eventually discovered to become

factual. Nevertheless, we're all being

lied to daily, hourly, and even by the

minute. Just turn on the television,

open a newspaper. How many stories

are created to blind us all with the real

truth? I'd say 99%.

Back in the 1990s, we were

brought to the dreaming stage,

emphasizing that dreams can only come

true living in America. However, that

seems to only happen with very few creative-related careers. Such being the next big musician, actor, or reality star. The next big author is similar to the next politician. It's all based on how much money you are willing to spend, only to make it up the extremely tall ladder.

The world we live in carries many broken barriers. This is quite clear to me, then and now. I only wish that others can see this. Perhaps one day, we will all laugh about how the *World Leaders* had created a fantasy world, and we learned the truth, without them wanting us to. Regardless of our reality situation, we must progress, this much is obvious. We need to change, we need to rise, we need to think for ourselves. All of these things are clear. Now it is up to you, the next individual who believes that I'm not crazy, nutty, or any other tag that the simulation is tossing my direction!

9

Without conspiracy theories, many of us wouldn't second guess our way of thinking. Thanks to books/movies like *The Secret*, some of us wouldn't reconsider *deleting* negativity.

Changing from a negative attitude to a more positive way of life, we would still be wondering around life being completely miserable. But what *The Secret* misguides many, is that *God* is here to help, God is the answer. But in reality, the best help is within ourselves. God has and always will be within our souls, it's the demons that we have to be weary of.

The voices from within our minds are sometimes not our own, and these can literally be a midfield. We agree to many things, because we're taught to stay on a certain path. Then one day, many of us wake up, and realize we're meant for greatness - but we just don't know how to get there.

Much of our personal goals seems flawless, until we run into the reality of these various broken barriers. Broken dreams occur, mainly to sift thru the ongoing explosions of real talent - not those who want to become the *One-*

hit-wonder to make it rich.

The folks like myself, who are in it for the long haul, are the ones that eventually make it big - unless some horrible way of death occurs, and ends it all before we discover our dreams becoming realities.

Sifting through the hundreds, if not thousands of threads on Youtube.com, I had finally come across a theory based on Trump, and the elections since the late 1960s.

The theory is, that Donald Trump was not only cloned once but twice, since his rumored-to-be-death in the mid-1980s. *They* claim that one

clone wears a blue tie, and the other,
wears a red tie. This theory would
explain (what seems to be) his split-
personality disorder! Perhaps there is
even a third clone, which would be the
one responsible for all of his *Tweets* on
Twitter.com.

The second theory, is that after
1967, computers are the reasons to
place blame with all elected Presidents;
and as I've concluded previously, *Our
Votes Don't Make Any Difference!*

Both theories were stated by
"Dick Gregory." Who he was, doesn't
seem to make any difference (a
comedian/human rights activist).

Nonetheless, he had proved many of theories, including both said theories, in interviews provided by his interviewee, on Youtube.com. Which I highly recommend you all to check out *Dick Gregory*.

The following three conspiracy theories I have uncovered on the web - which I too have considered myself, before coming across, which you may, or may not have heard of:

1) The CIA had invented a weapon causing fatal heart attacks. Dating back to the 1960s - 1970s.

2) CIA spied on, and used the media at their own disposal, dating back

to the 1970s.

3) The CIA used & tested LSD, and other various hallucinogenic drugs on Americans. This theory was thought of dating back to the 1960s; around the time MK-ULTRA had been created.

During these top 3 theories-to-be-proven, I had come upon an article from Canada. Which was discussing a Professor who had invented a machine that was named, *"Gay-Dar"*. Apparently, Canada was in fear of sexual orientation, in the 1960s - 1970s; which perhaps, they must've been led to believe that being gay, was somehow a contagious disease?

Alright, get this. I just clocked out of work - for my lunch break - at noon, July 8th, Saturday, 2018.

I got into my car, to head a home (a 7-minute drive, by the way). A mile into my drive, however, sounded as though a helicopter was directly over my car - even though I saw nothing above thru my moon-roof. I tilted my side mirror - on my side - and pointed towards the back wheel, on the drivers' side. It was wobbling, if you had guessed it.

I decided it would be best to turn back to my work-parking lot. I drove at slow speed, and finally had arrived. I pull the parking brake up, and jumped out, frantic - as you could imagine. I check the tire, and had noticed immediately that the lug nuts were loose. I touched one, and the damn think fell to the ground! All five lug-nuts were about to fall out.

After I tightened the lug-nuts on this wheel, I then checked the others. All 3 wheels were absolutely perfect. Therefore, it brought me to the conclusion that somebody deliberately had messed with the lug-nuts, in order to "make it look like an accident." This isn't the first time, either.

Two months ago, my car (the said car stated previously was my wife's, even though I was driving), had been tampered with as well. I was about to leave for work - luckily on her day off - and before leaving my trailer park, I noticed right off the bat, that my brake pedal went straight to floor; which I knew my brakes were bad, but I hadn't had any issues with the brake lines. Weeks' prior, I had an estimate on the brakes, and the mechanic said that the brake lines were fine. Therefore, it brings me to my conclusion: somebody had attempted twice this year on my life. But why? I'm a "nobody", not one that stirs shit up, except in my books...

My job is working at a low-level gas station, which I've hadn't have had any angry customers in the last few months - not death-causing worthy, that is.

If you - said hit-man, are reading this:

It's clearly not my time to die, leave me be, as I am nobody famous, nor am I attempting to be. Whatever the reason, <u>Mr.</u> Hit-man, I am sure it's not that big of a deal, so

just walk away, already!

10

There are two main types of people. Those that lead, those that follow. Those of whom follow, are generally runners - the type that runs when there are issues they cannot seem to face, in order to move on.

Leading is not an easy duty. Being a leader - not in a managerial way, is the most difficult role, like authors, for example. Many of us are leaders, but there are also those who attempt to rewrite what has already been written, to lead those that stray. Nevertheless, when we live in a country filled with *Broken Barriers*, it's about that time to lead those in worry, hurt, and the fearful. The reason, is to help those to leave the worry, fear, and pain behind. Not a physical pain, but all emotional. That's where I come in, I am here to help you better understand that the world isn't *Full of Sunshine & Rainbows*, and that our world *IS* here to harm us. It's left to us, to tackle these evil doers, and escape the madness, even if it's only for a short period of time.

I serious question I would like to leave you considering at the end of this book is this:

When a woman is carrying a baby within her womb, and with all the doctors' appointments she is led to believe that she must attend...Does a doctor ever sneak an injection in, to make "her" future child great? Or is "her" future child already born with the genetics to make "her" future child great. Is "her" future child going to be the next lead singer of The Beatles, Prince, Tupac...Or the next actor like Ving Rhames, Nicolas Cage, Susan Sarandon, Tom Cruise, Charlize Theron, Jennifer Lawrence, Julia Roberts...The next President, author, inventor, and so on.

I would like to thank you for reading this title. If you are new to reading my books, I highly suggest (if you enjoyed this book) to read other many titles I have provided my past, present, and future readers.

If you would be so kind, please leave a review on Amazon.com (or where you purchased this book), and also on my FaceBook page. If you have any questions, please contact me at: bobby.simonds@gmail.com.

1) A twist in travel: Fate (sci-fi)

2) The incident of 12/6/14
   (nonfiction)

3) A twist in travel: Scientific
   Wastelands (sci-fi)

4) J.J.'s Rhymin' Adventures:
   The Complete Series (kid's
   poetry)

5) The True Masterminds of
   Manipulation: Volume 1
   (nonfiction)

6) The True Masterminds of
   Manipulation: Volume 2
   (nonfiction)

7) The True Masterminds of
   Manipulation: Volume 3
   (nonfiction)

8) Living with Mild Cerebral
   Palsy (bio)

9) The true masterminds of
   manipulation: The complete

series (nonfiction)

10) An angry memo: attention all humans (nonfiction)

11) Mind boggling experiences of the weird & strange (nonfiction/paranormal)

12) Missing my dog, my best friend: Ginger (nonfiction/self-help)

13) Don't mind the little things! (nonfiction/self-help)

14) Where are all the good drivers? (nonfiction/self-help/educational)

15) Puggle fun with Ginger (picture book, young children)

16) Do you have what it takes to become the next

great author?
(nonfiction/self-
help/guidance/educational)

17)   Family in Ruins: The
loss from a suicide
(nonfiction/self-
help/guidance)

18)   What is banned in
America: Volume 1
(nonfiction/awareness)

19)   Risen from the Ashes:
Untold Truths & Theories
(Volume 1; Political
Awareness/nonfiction)

20)   Empty Conversations:
Dear Dad
(nonfiction/grievance)

21)   Risen from the Ashes:
You be the judge (volume 2;
nonfiction/political
awareness)

22)   Risen from the Ashes: Surrounded by Stupid's (Volume 3; nonfiction/political awareness)

23)   Risen from the Ashes: Living in an Unjust Society (Volume 4; nonfiction/political awareness)

24)   A Twist in Travel: The End is Near (sci-fi/series)

25)   Risen from the Ashes: Broken Shackles, Part 1 (Volume 5; nonfiction/political awareness)

26)   Where are all the good drivers? Driving in Upstate New York (Volume 2; nonfiction/education/awarene

ss)

27)	Risen from the Ashes: Broken Shackles, Part 2 (Volume 6; nonfiction/political awareness)

28)	Risen from the Ashes: Broken Shackles, Two-Fer (Volume 7; nonfiction/political awareness)

29)	A Twist in Travel: The Final Journey (science fiction/action; volume 4; end of series)

30)	Risen from the Ashes: Identity Crisis (nonfiction; volume 8)

31)	Risen from the Ashes: The First 8 (nonfiction; volume 9)

nonfiction; self-awareness)

44)	Bobby's Creative Photography Series: Volume 1 (nonfiction; photography)

45)	Bobby's Creative Photography Series: Volume 2 (nonfiction; photography)

46)	Bobby's Creative Photography Series: Volume 3 (nonfiction; photography)

47) Toxic America: Broken Barriers (Volume 5; nonfiction; Self-awareness)

Thanks Again!